Viewpoints:

D. L. Arber

2

Contents

No part of this story may be reproduced, distributed or transmitted in any form or by any means, or stored in a database or retrieval system, without the prior written permission of the author.

About the Author

D. L. Arber, writer, actor and poet, was born in Illinois and grew up in Colorado. He is a 2005 graduate of the University of Northern Colorado in Theatre Arts. As a student he performed in numerous school productions and also participated in New York University's summer theatre program. Following graduation he worked on stage, both as an actor and a producer, and in television in New York and Los Angeles, before returning to Colorado. In recent years he has been involved in writing both short stories and poetry, and now this political work.

Viewpoints

Introduction

Some days I find America to be just the place for freedom and justice; other days, I find it to be full of lies, greed, deceit and peril. Looking out my window in the foothills of a mountainous neighborhood in the state of Colorado, I have been presented with many different issues with this years presidential race and it has lead me to my computer where I have chosen to write something regarding the issues that many Americans face, not just I alone. Watching two very different presidential candidates on the television duke it out under such topics as immigration, global warming and terrorism, just to name a few, has been at most, tiring. However, it has brought me to the opinion that since I am a registered voter, I have my own opinions on different issues and I also have some direct experience with others. It was time to explore each issue in a more specific realm, so that's just what I plan to do. Among the many topics that America struggles to deal with, one thing is for sure; it is we the people who makeup the values, the opinions and ultimately the direction that America's future takes which is why being informed is of utmost importance.

This list is long, but distinguished. This paper is filled with topics from immigration, from abortion to gay rights. Scribbles line the page and there are question marks as to what poses threats to our freedoms and also what inhibits us a nation to move forward. Holding us back is never the issues themselves, but what these issues mean in our lives and how personally they become intrusive and no longer fluid in our natural lives. Issues like racism and poverty only come up because the issue itself exists and begins to affect the lives of more than just a single individual and over time these issues become a matter of national interest. Watching a news program and also reading a newspaper, anyone can get a sense of what the United States is facing at any given moment. The people affected, the places of destruction that communities distraught and the states that harbor all of the laws that pose change to the people of each city in the country.

Capital Punishment

The first line on my list is an issue that when brought to light is quite a serious one with many complications. The death penalty is something that is taken into account when a person kills another in a community. then the state takes over and decides what happens to the killer. The state ultimately decides what happens to the few that carry out these horrible acts of violence and bring the issue to a close in a number of ways. The death penalty is frowned upon in different states across the nation, but then in others it is allowed. The last I checked, capital punishment is used by 32 states across the U.S. and is a primary source of punishment for those states. When a person or people commit a crime, these states decide if it is serious enough to be brought to light and to use capital punishment against them. When a crime is committed in one of these states, where capital punishment is legal, and then the criminal ultimately faces death.

People that know me know I am really not a violent person, however, those that just meet me I have found to be concerned or weary about my actions. I personally do believe that the death penalty should be a valid form of defense and that actions carried out by an individual should be ultimately punishable by death. Now, I do believe in God, and I do think that he plays a part when it comes to the decisions that are made among the state, because as you may know it is one of the Ten Commandments that state that thou shall not kill. However, many people believe in the fact that is one commits a crime that though shall be dealt with as they dealt it to begin with. An eye for an eye as scripture on the mountain puts it. It states, "An eye for an eye and tooth for a tooth." Mathew 5:38-5:39. When one is faced with a decision to make based upon the

evidence, in my current state of
mind it seems to be a correct
response to crimes committed.
We live in a civil society
though, and this does not mean
when a person breaks a car
window that you should simply
find that persons car and go and
break their window. As many
mothers may have said at one
point, if a man jumps off a
bridge does that mean you should
follow him and jump off that
bridge as well?   In the Sermon
on the Mount, Jesus urges his
followers to turn the other
check rather than seek any legal
steps that go along with the
crime committed. The death
penalty is the states way of
deciding what will happen to

those people that commit such terrible crimes. When one is presented with a murder, the state is going to use the rule of retaliation and present the death penalty in return to those. With a simple quote from the bible you can see what religion states and then what the separation of church from the state decisions have done and do to our country. There are many issues here, and I believe that when it comes down to the death penalty, a federal and state run penalty, that in an extreme case, like an act of murder, it should be carried out.

Human Rights

Scribbling along, I have found many of the issues that I think of, surround those of the minority population and those that have not been given a great deal of wealth throughout their lives. This brings me to an issue of human rights. There are many different levels to the issue of human rights, whether they are gay, bisexual, transgender, and or lesbian rights. In this century, as you may not know I was born in the 20th century, there have been new laws put into place and as of recently a law stating that a transgender person, a person born as a girl who identifies as a boy for example, or the other way around, would be able to use the bathroom of their gender identity, the identity they were given at birth.

These new laws are have been around for many years, the ideas dating back to the 16th century, but more recently they have are brought to the forefront of America because for one, there will probably be an issue on this years voting ballot and also because again these are the issues facing individuals across America. These laws that are brought to congress and the senate arrive because someone, an individual, in a city and county in a state in the United States has had a problem with this being that they are and then slowly their individual issue has come to light in a public forum somewhere and slowly made its way to legislature. I stand firm on the fact that equal rights means just that, equal. I think there are a number of communities across the nation in different cities that have these issues and many of the people seen in the news have been fighting for these rights for the individuals who can't fight for themselves, for those that need a grandstand of people to be on their side, who need a sounding board of people that stand behind them, fighting for freedom and what is right. I have had my own experiences with gay men and women and simple human rights for everyone weather they be straight or gay or lesbian or bisexual is what we need. I do feel that these issues have begun to create a niche for themselves and I think sometimes it starts its own little revolution within the community to help those that have been discriminated against form a stronghold, or a group of those that all stand firm on one side of the fence. I have been known to be on the fence for a number of issues, but in understanding what each group, those standing with human rights are working toward, I do stand with them in helping to solve what communities across the nation have created within themselves, a place where these people are not wanted or are not valued as civilians and citizens, but in the past were persecuted against. These days in the beginning of the 21st century, these groups have fought to preserve their place and strength in the communities they serve.

Terrorism

The third scribble on the list I came up with that I have heard a lot about on the news is Terrorism. Watching the news about an hour a day, and seeing a newspaper on the weekends, even checking the online news sites, I see a regular stream or different acts of terrorism that appear. They have been going on off and on since that of September 11th, 2001, and they have penetrated the news programs since then. I, being a us citizen, uphold that which is sacred: to be an American. I don't condone any form of national or international terrorism. Barbaric acts of suicide bombers and mass shootings or killings made by terrorists, are definitely not something I stand for, and the majority of Americans who are concerned for their safety and stand for their freedom don't want to see the nation they love so much destroyed and infiltrated by terrorist acts. I believe the us military does a decent job protecting us from extremists, but I do know that it is in the news quite an awful lot and there is a chance that it might happen to locals and those people we love seems higher now due to the regular bombings in other countries and the willingness of these radicals to want to penetrate the us landscape.

Whenever I turn on the radio, I find news about terrorism, stories of women and children being killed. This is August of 2016. I think for the past many years these Middle Eastern countries have tried their best to enter the United States and make it known what they stand for, which I believe is no more than an attempt to put federal aid to use. The strength of the American people seems to withstand a lot of the violence and our will seems to overpower the terrorism in our schools and abroad. However it still happens and regularly I do

see many of the acts that affect
us all, emotionally and
physically and mentally in our
own lives. Seeing the regular
stream of Islamic radicals
across the world terrorizing
countries that has an effect on
us all, whether we believe it or
not; it prompts us to take
action against those that carry
out these acts and prosecute
them to the utmost extent of the
law, those that attempt such
acts inside the United States.
The issue of Terrorism has
always been in the American eye
for as long as I can remember,
but was not such a force of
nature and a problem to reckon
with since the most recent bouts
of the Islamic groups that have

been the recent center of attention with Americans.

As a United States Citizen, I do find myself worrying from time to time about whether or not terrorism will find a place in the American regions that we call home. It has in recent years. This makes me worry for myself in public places, in movie theatres and places where I have seen such terrorism occur. National terrorism and international terrorism are two different things. The problem I have found is that it has become hard to trust Americans with guns and those with access to firearms, because there is always a chance that these people that have been trusted with a gun in the first place could ultimately turn against others in their own worlds that they have all created. Later on in the book, I will discuss some gun ownership issues that I have and have noticed and will bring to light my reasoning why we should not be issuing guns to people that have criminal records and have a past history of violence.

Terrorism is a very important topic in this year's election. Since the dawn of September, 11th 2001, it has been a regular issue on the ballot and with whom we elect for president. I don't believe

Americans should be allowing someone to come to office that may or may not jeopardize our freedoms as Americans making the United States an unsafe place to live. The candidates this year both claim to be out for safety of the American people, but we must watch close as to who will make the right decisions as far as which groups will be the focus of elimination across the world and locally. I stand with the candidate that ultimately will bring safety back to our schools and our workplaces and our cities.

Abortion

I scribble on a number of things, including a little notepads for a grocery list, and sometimes I will write something of meaning next to "orange juice." On my list today, the next issue I plan to discuss is abortion. Also, a serious topic in this day's world, I believe for one it is because we live amongst people who practice religions that don't believe in abortion. There are many different political standpoints, but abortion has, in my city, earlier this year, a news issue as there was a Planned Parenthood attack on a local clinic here where I live currently, in the state of Colorado. My scribbles came to abortion, probably because when I watch the hour of news each day I find different areas of importance in my own mind as well as issues facing others. I have never been married, I have never had children. Abortion is one of the main issues facing women today. The topic of abortion has been around for decades now, and continues to be a serious topic when it comes to issues of rape, incest or disease.

Many people believe it is a necessary way out to have the ability to change the course of life for a baby. Some believe there should be a way to abort a fetus, and others believe that there shouldn't. Simply put, my standing is that there should be a way for a woman to have an abortion, and there should be a safe procedure for doing so. I think there are doctors out there that don't want to perform such procedures due to their religious upbringing, but there definitely should be a place where a woman, in case of those mentioned above where it should be able to be performed.

Abortion clinics like Planned Parenthood have been in the news since the Roe V. Wade argument in 1971. There continues to be a debate on weather abortion should or should not be legal in 2016 and will probably continue in the coming years ahead. Abortion is a sensitive topic for Religious groups as well as both men and women, particularly for an expecting mother. It continues to be a discussion many of us have with our mothers as well as our daughters. I have not had much experience with the topic hands on, however I have had conversations with my mother and her view point that a woman should have the right to choose whether or not a woman should be able to have or need an abortion. I also take that view point. There should be an

option for women to have the
legal right.

With the mass shootings
that took place in 2015 at a
Planned Parenthood, I have found
that this city of Colorado
Springs, being quite
conservative in political and
religious views, that the man
that did the killing had come
out of a very right wing place
of mind and also had a history
of other charges living in the
state. He had his own reasoning
with the opposition of abortion
and was one of the reasons he
carried out the shootings. I
was there watching the local
news when it happened and I
watched in horror as the victims

were said to have died of gun shot wounds. There are a number of issues I have with the shooting, and again I will go on more about gun safety in the coming pages. To sum it up here shortly, the shooting could have been prevented if there were laws against people of his nature having a firearm or a gun in the first place. He also had a history of violence toward animals and past criminal charges. The shooting has a number of issues to it, one falling into the realm of the abortion laws we have in the U.S. and also it falls into being an act of national or domestic terrorism, which I discussed earlier on. Coming to a close, after all is said, at the end of the day, I believe that a woman should have the simple ability and right as an American to have an abortion legally and safely in the convenience in the city in which she lives.

Disabilities

Sometimes, my scribbles turn into doodles. I have a little drawing pad for all my doodles and I have even created a comic strip that is really not at all political. The next I will be discussing here will be about disabilities. This topic I hold close to my heart as I have been around people with disabilities for most of my life off and on and through my twenties and thirties I have seen different psychologists and most recently a psychiatrist that prescribes me a small pill to help my diagnosed case of Schizophrenia. The Americans with Disabilities Act of 1990 is intended to protect those with a disability from all walks of discrimination. It also allows for employers to make reasonable accommodations for a person with a disability. I have had a first hand approach to a disability. And I recently have come up with ways to work that keep me active, healthy and working in a manner where I can still stay productive. I know that there are many Americans with a disability of some sort, whether it is a physical impairment or mental disability, I have come across many people who have these differences in lifestyle and should be protected under law.

I only recently have had a mental impairment that I am aware of and thankfully it came at a time after the disabilities act had come into American consciousness. I have worked with professional psychologists over the past 15 years to finally realize what some people believe to be my diagnoses. Since leaving New York, the city where I lived for nearly 3 years, I have moved to a place where there are mountains, outdoor activities and a majorly different climate. I was suspected to have an onset of Schizophrenia when I was in my twenties, and have some different things happen to my when it was then. Starting when

I was very young, I have always
had a tough time getting along
with the masses and I think it
was because of the cut and dry
methods there were to life.
There were categories, and there
were set in stone ways of living
that made me more focused to
sort of break outside the box.
I have noticed that much of my
upbringing has been in the arts
and I have a lot of my adult
life in the arts communities and
on set with different actors and
artists. I also have been in
professions where it was
entirely difficult to find work
due to the mass amount of people
and lack of work. At times I
have been over worked and

underpaid. It came with the profession I chose as an artist.

Only in the last couple of years in Colorado, away from all the media, the culture and the working artists, did I realize how much certain things mean to me, and what I was lacking. What I have found, in treatment, is that I enjoy a number of things like clean air, quality of life and my overall happiness. My health has increased being in a state where one can get outside and not be smogged out by traffic or busses. I have also found that a small city has its perks, and a large one has it's as well. But for me, I have found a smaller city to be better mentally for a number of reasons. I like the quieter neighborhood, the lower crime rate, the cheaper prices and the ability to be closer to my family. When I moved to New York, it was for business and the chance to get things moving in my acting career. I have acted in a number of productions from stage and theatre, to television and film, I have had the privilege to be apart of numerous productions. How this all ties into having a disability I will let you know. Simply living in a different part of the country among different people had a great affect on my mental health.

Being around loud noises all the time, people who potentially could take my money, and people who have domestic criminal charges made a big difference to my mental health. I chose never to go back unless I don't have to struggle. I have chosen to move back to Colorado, to be closer to my family, to be in a cleaner place and among people that don't have as many problems as those in larger cities do. I would love to do theatre again, and may end up even writing a script or play at some point, but for now I am focused on my mental health as a human being. Colorado has brought me back to me and helped me find out what I truly love about life and work

and my own personal happiness.
I like the mountains and blue
skies and it is less expensive
to live here than other cities
in the country. For now, my
mental health is priority.

It turns out that my mental
health qualifies as a
disability. So to those out
there that also have a mental
impairment or a physical
disability, I fight for those
that have these setbacks and I
proudly stand up for the rights
of the disabled. I am very
happy that there are rules for
disabled workers and rights have
been given to the disabled. It
means that we too have rights.

When it comes to our next president, this year being an election year, and because I have now a designated disability, I chose not to support a candidate who mocks the disabled and this year, that candidate is Mr. Donald J. Trump. He has been in the news as of recently that showed his true nature and it seems to me and others that have watched him this far, he may be an unfit president. He has made comments about disabled people that offend many people of this country.   It is not right to offend, and he should make amends. I don't believe it is going anywhere in this day and age, but nonetheless, I think the disabilities act should continue to remain in place for those that need it and again for those that can't fight for themselves.

Immigration

Scribbling lightly, I come across an issue that is dear to many of our hearts, to those of us that have migrated or moved from one place to the next but inside have a nationality or background that makes moving here that much more great. Immigration, a topic that is near and dear too many of us is a something that I do not think about everyday, but I do find time to think about it in my upbringing, and also a topic that rings true because I know that my nationality and history is not based in the united states. I have a nationality that stems from Russia, from

Romania, from Greece, Germany and England. My parents are both a granddaughter and grandson that come from England and Germany. Myself, I was born here in the United States, but in the back of my mind know that my relatives are from across the world and it is a privilege to be here. Growing up I have definitely been apart of the American landscape, with to start with, my automobile is made in the USA. I have never been outside of the United States, but I have been close. I have been to both coasts, where there were people from all walks of life and also from all different nationalities and backgrounds. Even today, I run

into people from all over,
wherever I go and meet people
from all different backgrounds.
Which, to me, looking back at
the time I have been where I am
currently, at the base of the
mountains in the state of
Colorado, it just goes to show
you that now matter where a
person lives, he will come
across all different types of
people from all walks of life.

Since I started high
school, I have noticed the
constant change of people from
all over, and in the city where
I grew up there have been
working people from different
avenues and backgrounds that I
have only grown to know and

understand. Immigration is a
topic that is on all of our
minds and many of us, when
looking back to their parents
and or grandparents or great
grandparents will find someone
that has moved here from another
country across the world to find
a better way and free way of
life in America. I am of the
generation that has grandparents
that have moved here from Russia
or from Greece or England in the
late 1800's. Not many people
can say they have distant
relatives that are either still
living or have passed away that
immigrated here as young people
in the 1800's or early 1900's.
I feel that it is a blessing to
be living in a country where

there is freedom, especially when turning on the television only brings war, crime and unrest from nations and cities across the world.

We should all rejoice in the fact that we have this freedom given to us simply by living in the United States. It all come with a price, but that price is something we should be thankful for because there are worse things and places that one could be living in a 3rd world country across the globe. We all have been given the gift of freedom in this country and I am here to say that it shouldn't be taken advantage of, and should be cherished. When living in a

place that has such a vast
amount of freedom, being a
nation of immigrants I can say
that having a nationality that
is a amalgamation of different
cultures and backgrounds, I am
happy to say that most of
America embraces those with
these traits and I am proud to
live in a place where our
differences are accepted as
neighboring qualities we all
have to give and learn from one
another.

Racism

Now, many of the cultures that are in the news lately have been spawning outrage because there is a racial divide when it comes down to who is right and wrong, who cares about who, and where the unrest is coming from. There have been many years of different racial divides in the United States. Today's news reads a headline about a movement from a black and divided group that believes that white people in America don't care about black people and they are causing riots and protest lines with many thousands of blacks walking for justice to their movement. They believe

that the viewpoints of whites
don't care about those of blacks
and that they are not valued in
the America that we all know. I
personally believe that these
movements are not needed,
because it causes for divide in
our country that simply living
their lives peacefully. I don't
see why protests and picket
lines bring equality. Black
culture has been fighting for
equality for many years and laws
that were created by whites in
the 1950's still have an effect
on the minds of today's black
people. I don't think there
should be marches exclaiming
their injustice. I believe it
is like teaming up among many to
prove to the other side who is

right and who is wrong. Teaming
up to form a line, most of the
time does not win the game, it
only creates more tension.
However, there continues to be
demonstrations. Daily I see
headlines about protests, or
inequality in the justice
system, however in the past few
years there has been a shift to
a more equal and less divided
culture and what I have noticed
is that there is less division
than in the 1900's because I
think many people are learning
from the previous generation's
mistakes.

     Racism has played a part in
America for years and has been
noticeable in all forms of

government, in our schools, and in the workplaces of many individuals. However, what I have noticed in my own experience is that there always have been people of different races when you are confronted with a diverse workplace. In fact it seems that the goal of many organizations these days is to attempt to have a diverse workplace, that it spurs growth. Not knowing for sure, but many people of different walks of life are proud to work in an organization that embraces equality. Surely it depends on where you live and the different parts of the nation, I find that where there is a will, there is a way to equality. In a diverse workplace people embrace the differences of many all to achieve a common goal. Racism, ceases to exist in a workplace of such different people and backgrounds, and for many companies that exist in today's business realm, it is not tolerated.

Personally, I have never come across much of a racial divide among those I have been around, worked with, spent extracurricular time with or gone to school with. Everyone has different needs and wants, but many of the places where I have met a black man, or an Asian woman, have been places where I was really there to mind

my business and work anyhow. I
know that today's white
generation seems to be
diminishing that I have heard,
and it seems that in the coming
years whites will become more of
a minority and less of the
majority. I personally have
differences of opinion but this
has only been word of mouth that
I can say, however I can only
bet that there is a chart or
graph and solid evidence backing
that theory up. Many of us in
this day and in the past find
our own and stick to those is a
match in their eyes to make.
For example, in searching for a
partner or a sole mate recently
on the dating sites and in life,
I have found my interest to be

for someone that is of the
similar background as me and of
a similar upbringing. It is
simply because I believe that we
look for like individuals that
we can bring into our lives.
Simply searching for someone
that matches my interests is a
difficult task; it is becoming
harder and harder to find
someone that fits the build of
what I am looking for in another
human being.

That all ties into Racism
because I am white and I don't
typically search out for a Black
or Asian person in my
subconscious thoughts. My
normal response is to seek out a
white and perhaps a European

person that doesn't have
something of a mixed background.
Being a single person, I have
seen many different people of
different walks of life and I
come down to understanding that
many of them, in my age group,
being 30-40, have already been
married and have had children,
and sometimes that has been with
a person of a different race.
It makes my wonder if these
people have had plans in their
attempt to sort of make the
world more racially mixed.   I
have found that searching for
many people, that it has become
difficult to find the match of
my dreams, because many of the
people are mixed to a point that
it becomes a culture of

differences instead of a culture
of similarities. In my mind, I
have been the one that has been
singled out, and I think it is
because everyone has chosen to
find someone and not be as
choosy as they should be when
finding a potential mate to
spend the rest of ones life
with. It seems that choosing
race as a factor when finding
someone to be with has become
something that is a last resort
for many and a risky behavior
for others.

Finally, growing up I have
lived and worked around people
of all different races and
understand what it is like to be
an individual among many that

are different. I am a Caucasian male and I have found myself to more and more be and live around people of different races and nationalities. I have moved a few different times to different cities for work, and more and more I am presented with different cultures and backgrounds. I find it interesting that black American's are more often attempting to be a role of power and authority when it was a white American in the role previously. I must say though for every one black person I see on TV, there are that many white people too. In today's world however, I find it even more difficult to trust anyone, and at the end of the day, race is not the deciding factor.

Poverty

Over the years I have seen a lot of different types of poverty. I have seen a person in my class, where I have gone to school who can't afford to eat lunch, or I have seen people with clothes tattered and holey socks and jeans. I also have seen people in my city struggling to survive in a community where there isn't much around. I have seen poverty first hand in a living situation in a large state where I lived for a couple years. Then I have seen poverty in the workplace where people can't afford to eat or travel to and from. Poverty exists in our schools and our

workplaces and it also exists in
our neighborhoods. I believe
that a person who has never seen
any sign of poverty in their
lives is truly blind to that
part of society and chooses not
to see them. Poverty exists for
a number of reasons too. Rising
gas prices, rising rental costs
of living quarters and of
expenses like food and goods are
contributing factors to poverty.
I personally am aware that there
are many people that live below
the poverty line in my city
alone. There are not enough
businesses to support the
population and because of this
many people become homeless or
can't afford their meals or
clothing or personal items

because these things have just become too expensive.

Growing up, I always had what I needed, but I didn't always get what I wanted. I know that there is a difference and having what you need and also having what you want is a matter of privilege. I think there are a lot of people that can get whatever they want whenever they please due to a job they have or a gift they have been given. However the majority of us still live day to day, with only a budgeted amount of money to live on. Poverty is and can be a result of ill education, or is subject to illness or is due to a tragedy in the family. I think there are many reasons poverty comes to light and I don't think it happens overnight. I do believe that there are choices that one can make to get out of poverty, but sometimes the surrounding factors in life overpower ones ability to dig themselves out.

Personally I have known many people on public assistance and welfare and I have seen the poverty in our communities. I believe that poverty is different to every individual experiencing poverty. Being in debt for example is one way that a person can slowly succumb to poverty as if they don't pay their debts and if they are in a

situation that requires them to
pay more than they make for an
item, then slowly they become
poor and fall below the poverty
line. There are situations,
that I don't personally know,
only because I have kept myself
working, and out of poverty for
my life as I have been to
school, been to work, and have
stayed away from crime and
trouble. Many people who live
below the poverty line are not
well educated, don't have a job
and could possible have had a
run in with law enforcement due
to crime. This is just a guess
on my part, and is perhaps in
many cases not the truth.
However, there are those that
fall into the category of living

below poverty because of lack of
income, again lack of education
and also due to an extreme
tragedy in their lives which
prevents them from working
regularly.

Where do I stand? I
personally have lived close to
the poverty line for some years
in between school and work, and
then I have lived well above it
for some time because I have
held full time positions with
local employers. I try to
budget my money as well as
possible and I do my best to
stay on the positive side of the
poverty line. Different things
I can't control, like recently
for example I have been living

in an apartment complex that has raised the rents when resigning their lease. By increasing rents, they begin to weed out the people that cannot afford to live at a higher rate, and pay the higher rent prices. The community is located in what is supposed to be a better part of the city, less crime and more quality access to outdoor recreation and open space. I ask myself if it is worth it, but I have lived in worse off communities in my time renting. I think there is a chance that many people would rather deal with a higher rental price than live among crime infested neighborhoods and also a place where there is a chance to be

the headline on the nightly
news.

Poverty effects many of us
and I think there is a chance
that there are many days where I
feel like less of a free human
being when I faced with
financial obligations that I can
or cannot control. I do my best
to fight off the effects of
poverty and make steps to create
a better and positive
environment to live in and
around. Sometimes, poverty
can't be controlled however,
when a person is in a situation
that swirls them out of control
into payments, or expenses that
send the person down a slide
that ends up below the poverty

line. All in all, I believe poverty can be avoided, if one takes the necessary actions to prevent it or to stop it in its tracks before it swallows them up.

Global Warming

For the past few years, I have been noticing the steady influx of advertisements and news media bringing the issue of global warming to the forefront of the world's consciousness. I believe it is broadcast on the nightly news as well as in science journals and in different environmental magazines.   I also have noticed it personally as the landscape of where I live has slowly gotten longer and warmer and it seems that at certain times of the year the world seems to be getting warmer in different regions across the planet. People in different news realms

have brought this issue to light
as there are many people across
the planet that are noticing
similar changes to the planet
and the landscape. Some
politicians do not believe in it
and then some are asking for
change in governmental forces
for the good of the planet. I
believe that global warming is
an event caused by human
activity. I believe that
although it may not be deadly,
it has altered our environment
in numerous ways and because of
it, the earth is changing and
global warming is simply the
earth's natural attempt to
balance out its atmosphere.

The first time I remember hearing anything about global warming would have to be in the first year of college which for me was around 1996. It has been some time since those years, but it was the first time I remember hearing about the changes coming to the environment in which I lived. I know that the idea of climate change and global warming has been around for some time, but there have been more groups taking hold of the idea and making it into a national and multinational topic. I took an environmental studies course at my university where I learned about the climate and the different changes affecting the earth in the past as well as the present. It also presented ideas as to what could happen to the earth in the future given a current graphs and information.

After looking further and watching the change, there have been daily news headlines in the news about different ideas surrounding global warming and also there have been presidential candidates this year in 2016 that have put it down and disregarded it as an idea presented to a nation of Americans. I want to make clear that climate change is an issue facing all of the world, not just one nation and for a person in power to disregard it like it is not happening, I will just say to look at the details of the differences in global temperature from the 1900's to today. Global temperature records made by the Met Office Hadley Center and Climate Research Unit, NOAA National Centers for Environmental Information and the NASA Goddard Institute for Space Studies show a climbing increase in global temperature since the year 1850. The average temperature beyond the year 2000 shows an increase of nearly a full degree. As stated by the MET Office online, "The three independent global-average temperature records show that there has been warming in the Earth's climate since pre-industrial times. The warming has been particularly rapid since the 1970s. The records also clearly show each decade since the 1970s has been successively warmer than the last, including the decade since 2000. Changes in temperature observed in surface data records are corroborated by measurements of temperatures below the surface of the ocean, by records of temperatures in the troposphere recorded by satellites and weather balloons, in independent records of air temperatures measured over the oceans and by records of sea-surface temperatures measured by satellites. Indirect evidence of warming can be seen in the reductions in Arctic sea-ice, sea-level rise, reduction in glacier volume and in phonological records, for example the dates on which leaves, flowers and migratory birds appear."

A simple example of what people have seen for over the past several decades show that there is most definitely a change in the atmosphere and that there is a change of temperature to the earth, and it has created a warming to the temperature of the earth over the most recent past. It has occurred more recently than before and what many can only attribute it to is human impact. Also according to The Guardian, an online news source, Global land and sea temperature was 1.11C warmer in April 2016 than the average temperature for April during the period 1951-1980. 1980 was nearly 36 years ago and it shows the changes that have taken place in the past few decades were stronger than those changes that occurred over the past several hundred years. There has been more growth recently than that of the past before.

I would love to go further in depth, but I know after reading many of the news headlines and stories that I am convinced there has been some change over the course of my own lifetime, which amazingly seems short compared to vastness of earth's timeline. I believe in the long range of things that climate change is real and that there is real truth to the differences of temperatures and records that the world has to show for global warming, temperature records and climate change. I will say that I don't have details of how much industrial change there has been over the course of the past century, but that there shows just in difference of the simple inventions and the industrial changes over the past 16 years since the turn of the century, I have many times over the past few years worried that if I were

to live in a coastal region,
that I may as well jump into the
ocean as if there was a natural
disaster, it would sure swallow
us whole. These are the worries
that some of the news media
provides us, and I can only
follow the facts which I have
read about, seen on the national
landscape and in different
journals and magazines that
exist. In the end of it all I
do feel safer living in a
mountainous region which is far
away from the possibility of
typhoons and natural destruction
like tidal waves and high enough
in the landscape to escape that
of nearby earthquakes. These
disasters, all created by the
natural urge for the climate to

change, I feel safer to be
closer to the clouds.

Gun Control

Scribble this and scribble that. I find that there are many topics that have come up in the global arena that are made more important by the news media. They seem to want to bring these topics to light as they then present the issues and it is up to the lay person to tact action. The same is true on the national scale. When there is an issue facing any American, if it is a large enough issue, it is brought to light by the news teams and the journals and the magazines. The topic of gun control is not something that is taken lightly by most Americans. People that

believe in the constitution
believe that a person has a
right to bear arms, the second
amendment to the constitution.
I myself do not own a gun. I
used to own a small rifle when I
was younger and it wasn't
bought, it was a gift from my
grandfather. I think a citizen
of the United States should be
able to own a gun, but I think
there are things that must be in
affect to protect other people
in the world besides the
everyday gun owner. I know
first hand to see all of the
problems scattered across the
news and to see all that happens
or can happen when a person owns
a gun. There are accidents that
happen that can be avoided by

simple rules and regulations
that go along with gun
ownership.

One thing that needs to
happen for the future of gun
laws is that there needs to be
mandatory background checks for
people that want or would like
to own a firearm. I think there
should be laws preventing the
purchase of a gun by people that
have criminal records, illness,
and minors. There should be
these laws because it protects
the lay person from people that
have these issues and would like
to solve the smallest levels of
conflict with the use of a gun.
I believe there should be laws
that enforce the safety of the

human population. I have seen
the news on a nightly basis, and
it seems the country has a real
problem with issuing guns to
people that have no business
owning one and are simply there
to use them for the wrong
reasons. I know it is our
constitutional right to own,
however, if you are a criminal,
have an illness, or are a minor
it should be a no way, no how
issue.

Thankfully, I have never
been around gun violence. I have
only seen it second hand through
the news and through the media.
I have seen it in the city
streets through the eyes of a
television and of a computer

screen. I have never been on the street where the violence takes place, as I know better not to steer close to the trouble. I have watched movies where the handling of guns is next to nothing, been very like second nature and has been broadcast like it is an every day occurrence. In fact, it seems like it is. Over the past year, there has been gun violence in the news pretty much every other month, if not more than once in a single month. When watching it makes me feel unsafe in my own city if there comes a local man with a gun. I have watched countless murders and gun violence take place on television and in the news

online and even in the
newspaper.

I am happy to say that I
have never been involved in one
of these occurrences. I choose
to stay away from those that
have temper, or anger problems,
which I have had when I was a
bit younger, but have learned to
think a little clearer in the
recent years as I don't want to
be there in those situations to
suffer the consequences.
Personally I have been known to
get a little angry at times for
things I am unable to have or
get in life like material
things. But I have found that
the most important things in
life don't require gun ownership

and that owning a gun is just a means of protection from those that have issues like criminal records, illness and minors. I will most likely never own a gun for the rest of my life, as I find myself doing other things with my time than providing myself with protection and or self defense from those that threaten us.

I believe that more Americans own guns due to terrorism and violence, than ever before. I don't think it is that important to own a gun for myself, as I wouldn't really know what to do with it. Law enforcement should be the people we trust and I am ok with them carrying guns. The majority of gun owners are law abiding citizens as I believe, it is those select few that abuse their privilege to use them. These same people are the ones who commit crimes and cause trouble in our cities, schools and workplaces. It is my hope that with a new president this year, that there will be new gun control laws and that there will be a chance to get the guns off of the streets. I remember a campaign in the 1980's when people were yelling on television about getting the guns off the streets. The attempts in the larger cities to curb gun violence and get guns out of our kids' hands were a

large part of the 1980's. I
remember those campaigns and it
seems that Americans are facing
some of the same issues today as
they were 30 years ago when I
was in grade school. It just
goes to show that America faces
some of the same issues today
than they did 30 years ago.

Homelessness

I have never been homeless, and it is due to a number of factors. I have had a strong support system most of my life. I also have been in school for many years and also have been employed. I can say that homelessness happens for a number of reasons, but I don't know the details of it, because I have never succumbed to it. I have noticed more homelessness in my current state where I live. I have noticed a more growing population of people who have fallen to homelessness and I think there a number of reasons why. I won't go into too much detail as to what I believe, but I will list a few things that I can think of.

First, I think that homelessness comes because there is a lack of money and facilities to house the people that cannot afford to do things for themselves. I think with age and income brackets that people live in there is always a chance that certain people, without income, without jobs, and without a means for proper housing, will all succumb to homelessness. It doesn't happen to everyone, but when you have a city that has a low percentage of jobs, you will find a population that has a higher rate of homelessness. Also, when a large percentage of people in the city come from a military background, I think there is more of a chance that the civilian population could have a short coming and fall to homelessness due to lack of jobs taken up by the military.

This is not always the case though. Homelessness comes from illness too. Many people who are unemployed or do not have money is due to illness of some kind. Some is due to the fact that there is simply no money to help a person get back on their feet. Luckily there are some facilities that help with getting a homeless person back on their feet. These places

provide shelter, clothing, and
food and job preparedness to
help the ones in need.

I am thankful that I have
never been homeless; however I
have come to a point, where I
live off of a fixed income to
support my expenses and basic
necessities. I don't think
there is a path to homelessness;
however, I believe drugs and
violence can lead a person down
that road. I hope that I don't
ever experience homelessness, as
I want to continue to live
happily and healthy. Also,
since many cities experience
these problems of homelessness,
thankfully there are facilities
like soup kitchens and places to

sleep for the homeless
population so they can get
themselves back on their feet.

My Point of View

There are many issues and topics that I could carry on about for a while. I covered some of the few that I have seen first hand or have been in this year's political news and I have tried to present my point of view on the topics discussed. I don't feel I have been intrusive, but I will let you be the judge. My main thought behind writing this article was to bring to light and flush out some of my ideas so that I don't stand on the wayside and watch the years news go to the birds. I have attempted to discuss responsibly the topics at hand and I am happy to have put on the table some fairly hot topics that that are regulars in this years news. I suppose what I am slowly finding out is that if I bring a topic to light, it is brought out into the open and discussed, rather than leaving it in the dark. My current situation allows for a little leeway in life and I am thankful I have the means to stay out working and keep busy in the landscape and stay in my current living situation. Bad habits can be just that, bad. It is important to stay on the positive side of life when it comes to the topics facing our nation and individuality.

ACKNOWLEDGMENTS

I would like to thank my family and friends who inspired me to put together this collection of works. I also would like to thank those students and teachers who have been an influence to me who gave me the perspective to write. Above all I would like to thank God, for making this all possible. Thanks to those who were there while I received my education, you are not forgotten.

www.ingramcontent.com/pod-product-compliance
Lightning Source LLC
Chambersburg PA
CBHW050037260726
48658CB00005B/1645